BODYWEIGHT WORKOUTS FOR MEN

SIMPLE AND EFFECTIVE HOME EXERCISES YOU CAN DO ANYTIME TO GET FIT AND STAY IN SHAPE

FRANCIS PAPUN

CONTENTS

SPECIAL BONUS!

Get this additional Free 30 Days to Fitness Challenge Book 100% FREE!

Hundreds of others are already enjoying insider access to all of my current and future full-length books, 100% free!

If you want insider access plus this Free 30 Days to Fitness Challenge Book, all you have to do is **click the link below** to claim your offer!

https://mailchi.mp/1085fc44d91b/bodyweight-workout-for-men

INTRODUCTION

Are you looking forward to staying in shape and building your muscles? This ultimate guide will teach you about home workouts you can do without using any gym equipment.

You will learn how to stay fit, be healthy, and eat properly.

This book is suitable for men and women, but I will focus more on men (aged between 20 to 50) who want to perform effective bodyweight exercises in the comfort of their homes. You will be able to learn how to do the right exercise and work for different muscle groups.

In our first chapter, you will learn why you need bodyweight and strength-training exercises. You will also learn the basics of nutrition and incorporate the right diet with the right type of activity to stay fit and healthy.

You will also learn how to develop your workout plan and choose the right type of exercise to develop a particular muscle group. You will also learn how to determine what works for you based on your fitness goals and level.

With your fitness goal in mind, you will also be able to determine the number of reps you should do for each set and how many sets per workout. This approach ensures you have a balanced workout plan that works your whole body.

In this beginner workout plan, you will learn about different exercises that target your arms, neck, shoulders, chest, core, lower back, thighs, and leg muscles. These types of exercises will strengthen your body, increase flexibility and make you more balanced and stable.

There are many health benefits from doing bodyweight workouts. Keep reading to learn more about body weight and the different types of workouts you can do to keep fit and improve your wellbeing.

BODYWEIGHT & STRENGTH-TRAINING WORKOUTS

ARE YOU LOOKING FORWARD TO BUILDING YOUR MUSCLES and staying fit? There are equipment-free bodyweight workout routines you can use to build your muscle mass and strengthen your cardiovascular and nervous system. You don't need any gym equipment to work out.

You can do the workouts from anywhere, so there is no excuse. Being on the road or a vacation with no place to work out and no equipment to use is no longer justification for not working out. You can easily do the workouts in your sitting room, garage, and even in your office—no need to subscribe to any gym membership fee or buy expensive training equipment.

Bodyweight training can help you:

- To effectively lose weight
- To build strength and body endurance levels
- To reduce the risk of injuries on your joints, ligaments, and other body parts.

BODYWEIGHT EXERCISES

Bodyweight exercises, also known as calisthenics, are a form of strength-training activities that rely on your body weight to provide resistance to the movement. They are intended to increase your strength, fitness, endurance, speed, flexibility, and balance.

Some exercises, such as bending, pushing, squatting, twisting, and more, are great for bodyweight training. You need just a little space to do most of these exercises.

Although you'll need some equipment for a few of the following workouts, most of them do not need any equipment. For the exercises that require a piece of equipment, you can utilize a common item in your home.

Bodyweight exercises are more convenient and deliver positive results. However, if you're looking to build muscle mass, you need to do the right at-home exercises and do them in quick progression to make the muscles more explosive.

WHY BODYWEIGHT EXERCISES

1. Time efficient

If you want to improve your body composition and stay fit, you don't have to spend more than 2 hours exercising. Bodyweight training is highly effective even when done 30 minutes daily.

All you need is high-output exercises, such as plyometrics and strength training, with little breaks between the exercises. You can easily transition from one movement to the next with little rest.

Doing short and intense workouts can yield better results!

2. Cost-effective

Bodyweight training requires only your body and the working space the size of your yoga mat. You can begin your exercises right at home without spending anything.

Some of the low-budget equipment you may need to aid in your exercises are sneakers, a resistance band, and a skipping rope. Although, these are optional.

3. Increase your flexibility

Bodyweight exercises work on your whole body, thereby making your muscles more flexible and improving the health of your joints. A full range of motion ensures the free movement of your joints and reduces injuries related to workouts.

4. Highly scalable

Bodyweight movements are ideal for everyone. Whether you want to stay fit, are in sports, or are weight lifting, you need bodyweight training exercises. You can make modifications to your workouts by using sturdy objects in your home. For example, using your chair to do squats or burpees.

With time, you will be able to build your strength and improve your motions, and you will no longer need the support of the objects.

5. Combines cardio and strength training

Combining strength-based movements with bodyweight movements, such as push-ups, mountain climbers, and burpees, will keep your heart pumping, burn more calories, build muscles and boost your strength.

6. Increases your balance

Increasing resistance while doing exercises will result in increased balance. For example, mastering how to do an advanced single-leg squat leads to improved body awareness and control. Finding your balance during your workout exercises helps you remain flexible and more independent with time.

7. Safe

Bodyweight exercises are safe to do, regardless of the type of exercise, age, gender, and level of fitness. Simple bodyweight movements can be used for rehabilitation to reduce aches or joint pains.

Doing the exercises regularly will leave you with healthy joints and bones. You will also have a lean muscle mass.

8. Better results

Bodyweight exercises engage several joints and muscles in each movement. Exercises, such as push-ups and lunges, result in measurable results. These exercises are more effective and offer excellent athletic performance.

Bodyweight exercises are more convenient and have endless variability. You can decide to do light movements or go hard. You can easily adjust from doing high-intensity sessions to doing a recovery walk. So, with various types of exercises, you can achieve your fitness goal.

The level of customization of these types of exercises is what makes them more preferred. You can always get what you need and when you need it.

You can also incorporate strength training into your bodyweight workouts to improve your performance. Based on your goals, you can use these workouts to stay in shape and improve your health and well-being. Bodyweight and strength training is also suitable for athletes of all fitness levels.

STRENGTH TRAINING

Strength training involves physical exercises designed to improve your strength and endurance. When done correctly, strength training can improve your overall health and well-being. For example, it leads to increased bone density, muscle tendons, improves joint functions, reduces injury potential, and increases ligament strength.

You can use your body weight or tools, such as resistance bands, to build your strength, endurance, and muscle mass. Implementing strength-training exercises into your workout routine will improve your performance.

Within just a few weeks into the exercises, you will notice some changes in your body. The exercises are helping you burn calories and achieve weight loss goals.

WHY STRENGTH TRAINING?

- **Strong bones**

Strength training enables you to increase your bone density and improve your overall stiffness to the connective tissue. It helps reduce the risk of injuries because it enables stabilization of your body upon impact with external forces

- **Improve your body image**

Those who do strength training report that they feel excellent about their bodies after completing the resistance-training program.

- **Reduces body fat and builds lean muscles**

Consistent training will increase muscle mass and the body's metabolic rate (the rate at which the body burns calories while resting). The higher the metabolic rate, the more your body burns calories and maintains the other functions of the body.

The body burns calories during and after resistance training.

When doing strength training, you should follow a proper nutrition plan to see measurable results.

- **Help develop a better body mechanism**

Strength training can boost your body balance, coordination and improve your posture. If you always find yourself falling now and then, you can include strength training in your exercise routine to improve your body's balance.

Your balance depends on your muscle strength to keep you on your feet. The stronger the muscle, the more balance you have.

- **Help manage chronic diseases**

Strength training has various health benefits for individuals, especially those with chronic diseases, such as diabetes. Together, the exercises, along with the right nutrition, help them control and manage their conditions. For example, strength training helps reduce arthritis pain.

- **Improves your mood and boosts your energy levels**

Strength training increases the production of endorphins that is responsible for improving your mood and energy levels. The exercises also have a positive impact on your brain functions and improve your sleep quality.

- **Improve cardiovascular health**

Strength training, together with aerobic exercises, helps lower the risk of heart disease, boost your blood pressure, and reduces hypertension.

PRINCIPLES OF STRENGTH TRAINING

To obtain the best out of your training, you need to focus on these four fundamental principles:

1. Specificity

The principle of specificity states that the stresses you apply to your body while training should be the same as that of your favorite adventure. For example, if you have limited time to train, you should focus your time on the specific disciplines you want to do, such as walking or cycling.

So, if walking and cycling are part of your training routine, you should focus on them only.

2. Individualism

Everyone is different, and our bodies react differently to varying types of training exercises in different ways. So, if a specific type of exercise doesn't work for you like it's working for your friend, don't worry about yourself. Someone can get better results faster than the other while doing the same amount of training.

Some factors, such as pressure at work or home, can affect your training and overall results. Therefore, doing some exercise with your friend doesn't guarantee you the same results.

3. Progression

When starting, you can use simple steps to work out your muscles. As your body gets used to them, you can increase your workload and the resistance you put your body through.

Therefore, progression involves small increments. For example, increasing the stress you put your body through. Stress consists of the frequency of the workout, the duration, and the intensity of the workout. For example, you can start with a 30-minute walk today, the next day, you do a 45-minute walk until you can take a 5-hour walk every couple of days.

4. Overload

If you don't have enough rest in between the training, that may result in overtraining. You shouldn't confuse this with overload, where you increase the workload and implement the right amount of rest after each session.

If you properly increase your workload training and the right rest, it will result in overload. So if you're looking forward to improving your performance, you can employ the overload technique and avoid overtraining.

BODYWEIGHT TRAINING TIPS FOR BEGINNERS

1. Make the best use of your warmup time

Before you begin your actual exercises, you can start up with a light warmup to prepare your body for the set of exercises. Doing a warmup will give you better results!

You can maximize your pre-workout time by doing stretches and 5 to 10 minutes of light cardio to boost your heart rate, as well as lubricate your joints.

2. Start with short and straightforward exercises

Start with a simple exercise that feels manageable to you. As you begin to build your strength, you can increase your workout intensity. If you started with five squats a day, you could keep increasing the number of squats every time you're exercising.

· · ·

3. Avoid training to exhaustion

Do not overwork yourself if you feel you can't complete a set of workouts. You can end it before you completely exhaust yourself.

CHAPTER SUMMARY

Bodyweight and strength training are essential for men who want to stay fit and build muscles. You don't have to go to the gym or use expensive equipment to achieve your workout goals.

Bodyweight workouts are also effective and efficient in building your muscle, increasing strength, endurance, flexibility, and creating balance. They also reduce the risk of injury and repair your body from the stress that comes with lifting heavyweights.

In the next chapter, you will learn how to get started with bodyweight workouts.

2

HOW TO GET STARTED

Staying in shape and having a healthy lifestyle is crucial. Doing regular exercises will help you achieve your desired results. However, doing the right exercises for your daily routine can be very overwhelming, especially if you're starting out or for those who exercise only a few times a week.

Further, incorporating workout exercises into your daily routine requires a lot of determination. You need the discipline to stick to your workout routine.

Getting started on your bodyweight-training journey will result in improved health and wellbeing. Exercise improves your mental ability, supports your weight-loss journey, and reduces the risk of chronic diseases.

Before you start any workout, you should:

1. Check your health

Consult your doctor or get a medical examination report before starting any workout routine to avoid any risk of injury during exercises.

· · ·

2. Create a workout plan

Once you make your decision to do regular exercise, you need to come up with a plan that includes attainable steps and your training goals. You can start with some of the easy steps to do and continue building on it based on your fitness level.

Use progressive training principles to achieve your goals; starting with simple steps and carrying them to completion will determine your success. Doing a simple program will help you build a strong foundation and progress from one week to the next.

Achieving smaller milestones motivates and increases your chance of success.

3. Make it a habit

Once you start your workout routine, stick to it, and be consistent. If you make your workout exercises a habit, you will easily maintain your workout routine for the long term.

For example, you can develop a simple workout routine that works all your muscle groups three or more days a week.

Schedule a daily routine of exercises either in the morning or after work and make it a habit of following it.

4. Warm up first

Before you begin your exercises, you need to warm up your body first. Doing a warmup helps reduce the chances of injury when you start your workouts.

You can schedule 5 to 10 minutes of cardio or other warmup exercises.

5. Aim to challenge yourself

When starting, concentrate on doing each set of exercises rather than how many exercises you're doing. You will have enough time to improve your strength and build muscle mass.

HOW MUCH EXERCISE SHOULD YOU DO?

You don't need to be an active or high-performance athlete for you to do daily exercises. You can start by doing 30 minutes of exercise a day.

The American College of Sports Medicine recommends 150 minutes of physical activity per week. The 150 minutes of moderate exercise can be reconfigured to 30 minutes for 5 days in a week or 2 to 3 sessions in a week. So, instead of spreading the 150 minutes throughout the week, you can have 3 sessions of 50 minutes each in a week.

It is also advisable to start with simple exercises and increase the exercise's intensity as your fitness level goes up.

Though you can make the exercises part of your daily routine for better health, including some rest is also essential for your body. If you don't give your body enough time to recover from the exercises' stress, it can increase the risk of injuries. Muscle strains and fractures can be caused by overstraining your body.

Too many exercises can also make your immune system weak, increase fatigue, create a hormonal imbalance and increase the risk of infections.

PLANNING YOUR TRAINING PROGRAM

Are you thinking of starting your fitness journey? Building your workout routine is the first step to achieving your fitness goals and maintaining a healthy lifestyle. Your workout routine should include the plans, schedules, and the type of exercises to do.

A good workout plan should help you lose weight, maintain balance, coordination, and reduce the risk of chronic diseases.

When designing your plan, you should consider your age, nutrition strategy, lifestyle, free time, and goals.

You can quickly build your training program in these 5 easy steps:

1. Determine your fitness level

To start with, you need to know how fit you are. This will act as a benchmark to compare your progress. Your flexibility, body composition, and muscle density determine your fitness level. You can keep the record for comparison purposes. You should also choose:

- Your heart rate before and immediately after walking a distance of 1 km.
- How long did it take you to walk for 1 km?
- How many modified squats or push-ups can you do at a time?
- What is your body mass index?
- What is your waist circumference?

2. Come up with your fitness program.

Come up with your bodyweight workout routine for each day. Factors to consider when designing your fitness program;

- **Fitness goals**: What are your fitness goals? Do you want to lose weight? Do you want to build muscle? Are you preparing for a sports activity? Stating your goal will help you to stay focused and help you determine your progress.

- **What exercises to do**: Based on your goals, you need to develop exercises that will enable you to achieve the goal. What activities can help you lose weight or build muscles? Keep it simple. If you're a beginner, choose exercises you can do 2 to 3 days a week.

There are various muscle groups you can work on. If you're starting, you can choose one or two exercises to work your upper body and three or four exercises to work your lower body muscles.

You can select the type of exercise to do based on how your body feels. No matter the set of exercises you want to do, you should start with a 5-minute warmup with light cardio.

After the warmup, do a set of each exercise, one after the other, and take a 1-minute rest after each exercise session. After a while, with your routine exercises, you can modify them to be more intense. Always keep a note of how your body feels. This helps you keep track of your progress.

The workout routine you choose should have at least one exercise that works on the following muscles:

- Quads to work on your front leg muscles.
- Butt and hamstring exercises that work on muscles at the back of your legs.
- Push exercises to work on your chest, shoulders, and triceps.
- Pull exercises that work on your back and biceps.
- Core exercises for your lower back and abdomen.

Building a workout routine that focuses on 4 to 5 exercises can help you in working multiple muscles simultaneously.

- **A balanced routine**: You have created a balanced routine to help you achieve your goals. Department of Health and Human Services recommends that adults do moderate aerobic exercise for 150 minutes, intense aerobic exercises for 75 minutes, or a combination of the two. You should spread out exercises throughout the week.

The more exercises you do, the more the health benefits. Even being physically active for a short period during the day can contribute to your improved health.

You should include strength training exercises at least two times a week to work out major muscle groups. Do a single set of activities at a time focusing on your body weight as the resistance. Do at least 12 to 15 reps, which are enough to tire the muscles.

- **Start slow and progress slowly**: if you're a beginner, you should start with short and straightforward exercises and progress slowly. Ensure the fitness program can improve your motion range, strength, and endurance to avoid injuries. If you have any medical condition, you should consult with your doctor.

- **Incorporate exercises into your daily routine**: How much time can you slot for your workouts? Sometimes it may be challenging to get time to exercise, especially if you have a busy schedule. For your exercise program to work, you need to schedule a time for the exercises just like any other appointment. Your time commitment can help you design an efficient workout plan. Try building activity in your daily routine to make it easier to follow the plan. For example, you can take a break while at work to go for a walk.

- **Include different activities**: including various types of exercises keeps boredom at bay. You can include activities like swimming, biking that reduces injuries, or overworking some muscles or joints. Alternating from one activity to the other will ensure you work on all the muscles.

- **Include high-interval intensity exercises**: This involves doing high-intensity exercises for a short time followed by a recovery period of low-intensity exercises.

- **Include recovery time**: You should plan out the recovery period to allow your body to recover. Most people do exercises for days continuously without rest and only stop when they have injured joints or muscles.

- **Put it on paper**: Having a written plan will encourage you to stay on track.

3. Assemble the required tools

Always ensure you are in the right attire for your workout. If there are tools you need to use during your exercises, you can prepare them. To start with, make sure you have the right shoes based on the activity you want to do.

For example, cross-training sports shoes are great for giving the support you need during the exercises while running shoes are lighter.

You can buy a yoga mat for some types of exercises and a tracking device. If you want to keep track of distance covered, calories burned, and monitor your heart rate; you need a tracking device.

4. Get started

After creating your plan, you're ready to begin your training program. When starting your workouts, keep these tips in mind;

- **Start slowly and proceed gradually**: Always include enough time for warmup before beginning the exercises. Include gentle stretching to allow you to cool down. Then pick up your pace and proceed for about 5 to 10 minutes without getting overly tired.

When your stamina increases, you can increase your exercise time. Keep increasing until you can do 30 to 60 minutes of workout.

- **Break down the exercises if you have to**: You can schedule several sessions per day instead of doing all of them at once. Doing short exercises more frequently can be ideal for those with a busy schedule. You don't have to spend the whole 30 minutes doing exercises. Several short session exercises per day have aerobic benefits.

- **Be creative**: Don't be limited to the number of exercises you can do. Be more creative! For example, if you have been doing routine exercises such as bicycling, walking all week. You can include hiking with your family over the weekend and other activities. If you enjoy doing a particular activity, you can have it in your fitness routine.

- **Pay attention to your body**: You should listen more to your body, how do you feel after the exercises? Do you feel short of breath? Dizzy or nausea? Your body tells you a lot about your health. If you have been pushing yourself too much, it's time to take a break.

- **Be flexible**: If you don't feel well after a day of intense workout, take a break of a day or two for your body to recover before you resume the workouts.

5. Monitor your workout progress

After 3 to 4 weeks of your fitness program, you need to assess your progress. You can assess after every month to see whether you're on the right track to achieving your goal.

Sometimes you may notice you need to increase your exercise time to obtain measurable benefits.

If you didn't get the expected results, don't give up. You can set new goals and new activities to keep you motivated. You can also include your friend or family members to make the exercises more fun.

So creating your fitness program doesn't have to be hard. Proper planning and employing health habits will result in a healthy life and improved wellbeing.

HOW TO DETERMINE WORKOUT DAYS AND REST DAYS

To achieve your fitness goal, you need consistency. That is, you have to train regularly and over a long period. Therefore, you should create a program that is do-able and keeps you on top of the game.

The plan should have the right type of exercises and the rest. Come up with a simple schedule with all the activities to do throughout the week. This consists of 5 days of workout and 2 rest days.

The workout days should have a day of intense training followed by a recovery day with light exercises.

You should have 2 days for active recovery after intense exercises in the week. An active recovery day may involve doing exercises like going for a long walk, swimming, and Yoga.

HOW TO DETERMINE THE NUMBER OF SETS AND REPS TO DO

In every type of exercise you're going to do, you will come across the two keywords: rep and set. Rep (repetition) represents a single instance of a particular type of exercise, while a set represents the sequential number of repetitions performed—for example, 3 sets of 5 reps of push-ups.

A set involves completing a series of repetitive (reps) tasks that you do without stopping. For example, if you do 10 push-ups without stopping, you have done 1 set of 10 reps.

Choosing reps and sets sometimes can be challenging. However, your workout goals help determine how many sets and reps to do.

Rules to follow when setting up the reps:

- If you want to build muscles and burn fat simultaneously, the number of reps per set should be between 8 and 15.
- If you can do more than 15 reps with less difficulty, you can modify your activity to be more challenging.

Based on your goal, you can choose the number of reps you want to do per set.

- Doing reps in the range of between 1 and 5 help you build strength and super dense muscles
- Reps between 6 and 12 helps you build equal muscular strength and muscular size.
- While reps of above 12 help you increase your muscle endurance.

If you want to do high-intensity resistance, you can include 3 to

5 sets in your program. High-intensity resistance is excellent for men who want to improve strength within a short period instead of doing 8-10 reps.

When you're beginning your bodyweight program, you can start with few reps and increase the reps once you learn the movement.

SAMPLE ONE WEEK WORKOUT PLAN

From the above steps, you can come up with your training program. The example below is an easy to follow workout plan for a week, and it doesn't need any equipment.

You can adjust it based on your fitness level and goal. You can modify it to be challenging as you want.

Monday: 40 minutes of doing a brisk walk or jogging at a moderate pace

Tuesday: Rest day

Wednesday: 10 minutes of brisk walk followed by the following set of exercises. Rest for 1 minute after completion of each set. Don't rest in between the exercises.

- 3 sets of 10 lunges on each leg, 10 push-ups, and 10 sit-ups.
- 3 sets of 10 air-squats, 10 chair-dips, and 10 jumping jacks.

Thursday: Active recovery day with Yoga

Friday: Bike ride for 30 minutes or go jogging at a moderate pace.

Saturday: Go for a 40-minute walk, run or jog

Sunday: Rest day

CHAPTER SUMMARY

If you're planning to get in shape and build your muscles coming up with a training program will help you stay focused. A workout plan enables you to determine your fitness level and the goals you want to achieve.

Based on these two factors, you can come up with your schedule for the exercises to do. The plan will also help you determine what muscles to work out on each day and how long you should do the exercises.

You're also able to learn how to determine your workout days and the rest days and the number of sets and reps you have to do in each type of exercise. These factors will help you get started and ensure you achieve your fitness goals.

In the next chapter, you will learn how to strengthen your arms and triceps.

3

FIVE BEST STRENGTH-TRAINING WARM-UP EXERCISES

BEFORE STARTING ANY FORM OF WORKOUT, YOU NEED warm-up exercises to get your muscles started and ready for workouts that are more strenuous.

Sometimes, if you're short of time, you may be tempted to skip a warm-up section and jump-start your workouts. Doing this can result in muscle strain or increase the risk of injury. So, before starting any exercise, such as strength training, cardio workout, or sports, you must take 5 to 10 minutes to ease your muscles. The warm-ups help you achieve better results.

BENEFITS OF DOING WARM-UP EXERCISES

Doing a warm-up exercise makes your workout sections much easier and prepares your muscle for strenuous activities. Some of the benefits of warm-up exercise include:

- **Increased flexibility**: This makes it easy to do the exercise moves correctly.
- **Lowers the risk of injury:** Doing a warm-up before any exercise can prepare your muscles and get them relaxed. This helps reduce injuries.
- **Increased blood flow and oxygen**: Stretches and other warm-up exercises increase blood flow and give your muscles the nourishment they need for an intense workout.
- **Have less muscle tension and pain**: Having relaxed muscles enables you to move them more easily. This will result in less pain and stiffness. You will also be able to drive your muscle joints easily.
- **Gain better performance**: Getting your muscles ready for the exercises increases the effectiveness of your workouts.
- **Increased heart rate**: The goal of a warm-up is to easily increase your heart rate to cope with the increased heart rate during workouts. Increased heart rate gets the blood flowing.

DYNAMIC WARM-UP

You have probably heard of static stretching and dynamic warm-up and wondered what they mean.

A dynamic warm-up is a type of warm-up done to help start your workout routine. It prepares your body for more intense exercises. It focuses on making motions that are similar to the type of workouts you intend to do.

For example, you can do stretching movements that imitate movements, such as squats, lunges, or jogging.

Dynamic warm-ups help you build your mobility and improve your coordination. In return, this enhances the performance of your workouts.

STATIC STRETCHING

This is mostly done at the end of the exercises and helps calm your muscles after intense exercise.

Static stretching involves several stretches to help you lengthen or to loosen the muscles after intense exercise.

Stretches help improve your flexibility and boost your motions. Some of the stretches you can do include:

- Triceps stretches
- Hamstring stretch
- Hip flexor stretch
- Etc.

WARM-UP EXERCISES

1. Knee-to-chest stretch

Get into a standing position, then pull your right knee to your chest. You can use your hands to support your knees. Pull it as far as you can go and hold that position for 20 to 30 seconds. Lower your leg back down and repeat the same with your left knee.

This will stretch your hamstring and glute muscles in the back of your leg and increase your hip mobility.

You can also do this type of stretch while lying on your back.

2. Quad Stretch

Get into a standing position, then lift your foot toward your back. Grab your foot while flexing your knee. Hold into that position for 20 to 30 seconds and repeat the same with the other leg.

The quad stretch works on your quadriceps muscles and hip flexors in the front of your leg.

3. Triceps warm-up

This movement will help loosen up the triceps muscles. Get into a standing position and then extend your arms out to the sides. Keep your palms facing the floor.

Keep your arms straight, then start rotating them in a little forward circle for 20 seconds. Then rotate them in backward circles for another 20 seconds.

Extend your arms in front of you with palms facing upward. Then move your hand up and down for another 20 seconds.

Extend your left hand across your, then use the other hand to support yourself. Pull it as far as you can to feel the stretch and hold it in that position for 20 seconds, and repeat the same with the other hand.

4. Jogging leg lifts

Doing jogging leg lifts keeps your heart pumping and increases blood circulation. It prepares your body for an intense workout.

Depending on the available space, you can jog in place or run back and forth if your area allows you. You can start with a walking pace by lifting your knees to your chest and increase your speed as you warm up. Do this for at least 30 seconds to one minute.

You can also kick your feet behind and toward your buttocks.

5. Side Lunges

This warm-up exercise works on your lower body and relaxes muscles on your legs, glute, and hips.

Get into a standing position with your feet at hip-width apart. Bend your left leg to be in 90 degrees and extend your right leg straight.

Hold into that position briefly, and then switch your legs. You can modify this by including squats. While your left knee is in a bent position and right leg straight, you can lower yourself into a squat position. Do this for eight to 15 reps and switch your legs to repeat the same on the other leg.

CHAPTER SUMMARY

Doing a warm-up exercise is essential because, during the strength-training exercises, the muscles shorten and lengthen. If the muscles are not well-prepped, they're prone to tearing and pulling, leading to some pain.

A warm-up not only activates your muscles but also helps increase your mobility and your body's core temperature. Different warm-ups work on different muscles on your body and loosen the tissue around your joints. This makes it easier to do the movements in your workout and increase your efficiency.

4

BODYWEIGHT EXERCISES TO STRENGTHEN ARMS

Do you want to have ripped arms? Your weight is enough to work on your upper body muscles—no need to lift those heavy weights to strengthen your arms. Bodyweight workouts are useful for working on your shoulders, biceps, and triceps.

Most arm exercises with no equipment require you to use exercises that engage your core, such as planks and push-ups. This will allow you to work on both muscles at the same time.

No need for a gym subscription; you can work out those arms from anywhere. With a proper workout plan, you can quickly achieve your desired ripped arms.

The exercises require you to alter the position and angle of your body to make the right moves.

BODYWEIGHT EXERCISES FOR YOUR ARMS

1. Dips

Dips are essential for building your triceps and forearms. They also strengthen your pecs and shoulders.

You can use a dip bar, a seat, or sofa at home to do this exercise. Facing away from the dip bar or seat, hold the dip bar and lower yourself down until you make a 90° angle with your elbows. When lowering yourself at the bar, keep the chest out. Raise yourself back up to the starting position.

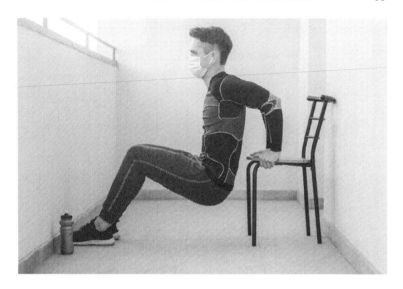

Ensure your neck and shoulders are relaxed. Walk your feet forward so that your butt is away from the chair's front edge and lower your hips towards the floor. You can keep the pressure off around your neck by looking at the ground in front of you, a few feet from you as you lower yourself.

You will find the exercise much more comfortable when your feet are close to the base of the chair.

Once you get the movement right, you can move your feet forward or lift one leg at a time as you make it more challenging.

To increase more strain around your pecs, you can bend your knees so that your feet are behind you.

If you want to focus on your triceps, you can extend your legs so that your toes point slightly in front of you.

2. Tricep dips with the lifted leg

Sit at the edge of a bench and place your hands on your hips so that the fingers point towards your feet.

Lift your butt off the bench and bend your legs to form a 90° angle.

Lift one leg straight and stretch it in front of you. Bend your elbow to an angle of 90°.

Push your back up to make sure your arms remain straight and repeat the step with the other leg.

3. Pull-ups

Pull-ups are an effective exercise for strengthening your arms, shoulders, and back muscles. In this type of activity, you use your hands to suspend your body and pull up. It is one of the most challenging bodyweight exercises, and once you perfect the move, you can quickly build bigger arms.

Leap up and grab the bar with your hands. Firmly grip the bar with your palms facing away and shoulder-width apart.

Hang on the bar with your hands fully extended. If your feet are still on the ground, you can bend your legs around the knee. Keep your core engaged and your shoulders back.

Slowly pull your body up until your chin is above the bar, then slowly lower yourself down until your arms are extended again.

Aim to do six to 10 pull-ups.

4. Chin-ups

A classic chin-up is similar to a pull-up exercise and even better working on your arms muscles than the pull-up. In chin-up, the palms are facing you! As a result, more workload is shifted to your biceps.

Just like in the pull-up exercise, grab the bar with your palms facing you. Extend your legs forward and your toes pointed, and then pull yourself up until your chin is above the bar. Slowly lower yourself down and repeat the movement.

5. Plank

Plank is a core-strengthening exercise, and it is similar to push-up exercises. You should maintain a position similar to a push-up for as long as you can in a plank.

It works on several muscles simultaneously and is one of the best exercises for burning calories.

On your exercise mat, get into a push-up position with the toes and forearms facing forward on the floor. Your elbows should be underneath your shoulders, and bend them on the floor to form 90°. Lift your knees, and keep your torso straight so that your weight rests on your forearms.

Keep your head relaxed, and you should be looking on the floor as you maintain your body in a straight line (that is, from ears to your toes) with no bending.

The plank not only works on your arms and shoulders but also engages your abdominal muscles, as well, thus, drawing your navel toward the spine.

Hold this position for about 10 seconds. Do not arch your back or tilt your neck. The neck should be in line with your body.

6. Up-and-down plank

This movement strengthens your shoulders, arms, core, glutes, and wrists. It helps in improving your posture and tightens your stomach.

Place your hands on the floor beneath your shoulders. Bend one arm such that your elbow and forearm are on the floor. Do the same to the other arm to form a forearm plank. Your elbows should be beneath the shoulders and alternative the hands to form a complete rep for a forearm plank.

Begin with the arm you started to back it up to form a high plank and do the same to the other arm.

Keep your hips and core tight as you do the movement.

If you find this movement difficult for you, you can put your knees on the ground to make the movement much easier.

7. Inchworm with shoulder taps

Inchworm exercise works on your shoulders, arms, and your core. Start by standing, then form a forward fold by bending your waist and stretch your hands until you touch the floor in front of you. Walk your hands out to create a high plank position.

Walk your feet forward, one at a time, to meet the hands and complete your first rep.

You can bend your knees slightly to make it easier for you.

Lift your right hand and tap to the left shoulder. Do the same, on the other hand. When doing that, engage your core and glutes to keep your hips in position.

Walk your hands back in and go back to your standing position. Repeat the steps.

8. Push-ups

Push-ups help you tone your arm and chest muscles. Start by placing your knees on the floor. Put your hands on the floor and move your feet back to form the plank position. Adjust your hands to be directly beneath your shoulders.

Pull your body from your heels and position yourself a few inches from the floor. Engage your core muscles to help your body remain straight.

Bend your elbows and lower your body until you're a few inches from the floor. Straighten your elbows to go back to your starting position.

If you find this movement too hard for you, you can start by assuming a standing position then place your hands on a sturdy chair or against a wall.

9. Triceps Push-ups

Get into a plank position with the hands underneath your chest and put your legs together. This will move the workload away from your chest to the back of your upper arms.

Position your hands such that your thumbs and index fingers form a triangle on the floor. Then, bend your elbows so that your body lowers a few inches toward the floor.

Hold on for a second, then extend your elbow back to the starting position. Ensure your core remains tight the entire time as you lower yourself toward the floor.

You can make this movement a little easier for you by dropping onto your knees and position your hips to be wide apart.

10. Elevated feet push-up

Elevated feet push-up is a modified bodyweight exercise that intensifies your movement. In this type of exercise, all your weight is shifted to your arms and chest.

This makes the exercise great for building your triceps strength and anterior deltoids. It also works on your pecs and core because you have to balance yourself so that the hips are not sagging.

It follows the same steps as a push-up exercise, but, in this case, you have to elevate your feet either on a bench or a sturdy box.

If you want to make the exercise a bit challenging, you can place your feet on a BOSU ball, which is slightly unstable.

11. Pike Push-up

Though a pike push-up exercise is tough to achieve, it is perfect for working on your shoulders and triceps.

This type of exercise resembles overhead lifting where you face upside-down.

To do this, get into a push-up position and then raise the hips so that the upper body maintains a vertical position from the hands to the hips. You can easily get into this position if you place your feet on a bench.

This exercise requires you to learn how to balance your body and scale down the weight load on your shoulders.

Ensure your hips are maintained up the entire time, and your fingers should be pointing directly in front of you.

12. Crab crawl

Get into a sitting position on the floor or your yoga mat. Keep your palms and soles of your feet on the floor. Ensure your fingers are pointing onto your heels, then lift your hips slightly.

Move a step forward by moving your foot and the opposite hand at the same time. Move the other foot and hand simultaneously. Each step you move forward makes one rep.

If you find it hard to move forward in that position, you can lift your hips off the ground for about 5 to 10 seconds to complete a single rep.

CHAPTER SUMMARY

Bodyweight exercises for your arms help in building arm muscles and increasing your strength. The above exercises work on your arms and upper body to increase strength without using any equipment or weights.

Bodyweight exercises of building your arms muscles reduce the risk of injuries. Some of the activities also target your chest, shoulders and core muscles.

The workouts not only strengthen your muscles but also help you burn calories and boost your metabolism.

In the next chapter, you will learn how to work out your neck and shoulder muscles.

5

NECK AND SHOULDER EXERCISES

BOTH YOUR NECK AND SHOULDERS ARE EXTREMELY MOBILE, and a range of motions can leave them unstable and more susceptible to injuries. And, for those reasons, you need to strengthen them.

Shoulder and neck exercises offer several benefits. The exercises strengthen the supporting muscles around the shoulder joints and enhance your posture and stability.

Strengthening your neck and shoulder muscles can improve your overall body structure. It also makes your shoulders strong enough to carry out your daily tasks without any injuries. There are also fewer chances of injuring yourself during the exercises.

Failure to work on these muscles can lead to impingement that limits your motion. The exercises make your shoulders more flexible and reduce stress on the shoulder joints.

Shoulder joints are very delicate because they're responsible for a range of movements. If you have weak muscles around your shoulder joints, your movement is affected, creating instability and injuries.

Therefore, the bodyweight exercises for your shoulders work on the rotator cuff (shoulder muscles) and the deltoid muscles. This helps prevent injuries!

BODYWEIGHT EXERCISES FOR YOUR SHOULDERS

These exercises allow you to tone your shoulder muscles while at the same time strengthening your ligaments and tendons. There are no weights required to do the exercises.

Shoulder exercises work on three types of muscles: Anterior deltoid, medial deltoid, and posterior deltoid. The anterior muscles are at the front, medial at the sides, while the posterior muscles are located on the rear (the back).

These exercises include:

1. Incline push-ups

Get into a plank position with your hands and shoulders elevated on a bench or box. Your upper body should be higher than your lower body. Lower your chest to a few inches above the bench, then push yourself back to the starting position, using your chest and triceps.

This technique works on your anterior deltoid and pectoral muscles. Your chest muscles are more active with incline push-ups compared to regular push-ups.

Ensure your shoulders and the feet are in a straight line, while at the same time your core and the hips remain engaged.

Doing three sets of 10 to 12 reps can give you better results within a short period.

2. Push-back push-up

Get into a push-up position, then move your feet wider than shoulder-width. Lower yourself to the floor with your chest, then push your upper body toward your heels rather than push yourself up from the floor.

When you push the upper body toward your heels, go back to your starting position—this type of push-up works on your abdominal, deltoid, pectoral and tricep muscles.

3. Plank to down dog

This type of exercise is excellent for working the rotator cuff. It increases your shoulder flexibility. Start by getting into a plank position with straight arms. Ensure your neck, shoulders, hips and ankles are in line.

Exhale, then lift your hips and move your head between your hands such that you create a straight line from your wrists to your hips and lower yourself back to the starting position.

Doing at least three sets of 20 reps can help you work on your biceps, hamstrings, shoulders and triceps.

Take your time to do the exercise; do not be quick when performing this exercise. Working on your hamstring muscles and calf flexibility will enable you to master the moves in this type of exercise.

4. Elevated pike push-up

Like in a normal pike-push up, you can place your feet on a bench, chair or box and start the exercise. You can also get into a downward dog position with your elevated feet.

Keep your hands wider than your shoulder width, and the fingers should face forward.

Bend your elbows, then inhale, and at the same time slowly lower your head until it is an inch off the floor. While at it, your arms should form a goal post shape and keep a slight bend on your elbows.

Exhale as you push yourself back to the starting position and straighten your arms. Lowering yourself in this elevated pike push-up works on your shoulders and triceps.

To increase intensity on your shoulders, you should place your hands wider apart than the width of your shoulders. Do not lock your elbows, as this can put some load onto your joints.

PIKE PUSH-UPS

5. Plank-up

Get into plank position and put your elbows on the floor such that you form a straight line from your heels to your shoulders. Tighten your core, then start by placing the palm of one hand on the floor to push yourself up, followed by the other hand until you get into a push-up position.

Lower yourself back to the starting elbow plank position and repeat the movement one arm at a time. You can perform one rep when you're up with both arms and down with both arms. This type of exercise targets your triceps and abs.

6. Wall walk

The wall walk is another bodyweight exercise you can do at home. It works on your abs, chest, back muscles and shoulders.

Get into a push-up position with your feet on the wall. Slowly back up and move your feet one at a time on the wall while moving your arms backward. Move until you're in a handstand position with your stomach a few inches towards the wall.

Slowly back down into the push-up position to complete one rep. Be slow when performing this type of exercise.

7. Crab walk

Sit on the floor and bend your knees. Your feet and shoulders should be wide apart and your palms behind you. Put your palms on the floor with fingers pointing forward.

Raise your hips off the floor and walk forward. Start by moving your left leg and right hand forward, followed by your right leg and left hand. Walk some steps, then use the same movement to walk back to your starting position.

This exercise requires you to engage your glutes and works your abdominal, glute, hamstring, tricep and quad muscles.

8. Reverse burpees

Stand on your feet wide apart (wider your shoulder width). Squat down, then lean forward with your arms out in your front. Put your arms on the floor like you want to do a push-up.

Get into a standard push-up position and ensure your body is in a straight line. Bend your elbows to lower your chest and body down to the ground.

Reverse your movement by pushing yourself up to the starting position. You can start up slowly until you get the correct moves, then speed up your movement.

You can advance your variation by jumping up after each rep and clap hands together over your head.

9. Handstand push-ups

The handstand push-up is an effective advanced workout for your shoulder muscles. You should be very careful when doing this type of exercise because a single mistake may result in an injury.

You can use a wall to support yourself and maintain the position as you perform the exercise.

Set a yoga mat or cushion against the wall, make yourself comfortable, and protect your head and neck.

Stand facing the wall, then put your hands on the floor with fingers spread to about 6 or 12 inches from the wall. Kick up until you get onto your hands. Place your heels on the wall for support.

Once you're inverted, straighten your body to be in a straight line and tighten your abs and, at the same time, squeeze your glutes.

Bend your elbows to enable you to lower yourself into the mat or cushion below your head. Control your body not to slam your head on the cushion or mat.

Once in the position, slowly extend your arms until you lock out your elbows to push your body back up. Do not rush with this type of exercise. Keep practicing until you're able to master the movement.

Handstand push-ups can be very difficult for a beginner, but with practice, you can get there. Before doing this exercise, you can start by getting into a reverse handstand position. And once you master how to kick-up into this reverse hand position, you can now advance to do handstand push-ups.

NECK-STRENGTHENING EXERCISES

If you have a weak neck and upper back muscles, you tend to have a head that sags forward. It will also stress out the cervical spine resulting in increased neck pain. So, exercising your neck muscles will help you improve your posture and get your head into a neutral position.

Having strong neck muscles help reduce the levels of energy

transmitted into the head during contact, and as a result, it prevents concussions.

The neck muscles include:

- Scalene muscle, found at the side of the neck
- Suboccipital muscle, found on the lower back of your head and at the top of the neck
- Postural muscles
- Upper thoracic extensors and deep cervical flexors

Most neck-strengthening exercises include:

1. Chin tuck

The chin tuck is the most effective neck-strengthening exercise that works on your postural muscles to combat any neck pain. This type of activity helps you strengthen neck muscles that pull your head back so that there is a proper alignment with the upper thoracic extensors' shoulders. At the same time, you will be able to stretch the scalene and suboccipital muscles.

To do this exercise, stand straight with your spine against a door jamb, pull your upper back, and head toward the door jamb. When pulling your head, ensure your chin and then pull the head until you touch the door jamb. Hold in that position for about five seconds and repeat the same 10 times.

When you pull your head and the upper back, you will feel some stretch on your scalene muscle that goes down to your collarbone. The scalene muscles, on the side of the neck, and the suboccipital muscle, found on the top of the neck, are very tight. Simultaneously, muscles at the front of your neck and upper back are very weak and require strengthening.

Once you have mastered the chin tuck exercise on a door jamb, you can easily do it while sitting or standing without any support of the door jamb.

You can do the exercise about five to seven times throughout the day.

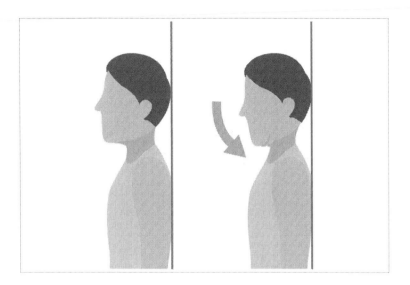

2. Prone cobra

Prone cobra is another strength-training workout that works on muscles around your neck, upper back and shoulder girdle.

To do this, lie on the floor with your face down. Place your forehead on a folded hand towel to make yourself more comfortable.

Place your arms on the sides with the palms touching the floor.

Move your shoulder blades toward each other and lift your hands off the floor. Move your elbows in, your palms out, and thumbs up.

Lift your forehead for about an inch off the hand towel with your eyes looking straight on the floor. Hold into that position for 10 seconds. Repeat the same 10 times.

Alternatively, you can raise your upper body with the arms on the floor and hold it in that position for 10 seconds.

3. Back burn

The back burn exercise enables you to maintain your posture. Stand with your back against the wall with your feet four inches away from the wall. The back of your head should be touching the wall.

Flatten your lower back against the wall and extend your hands to touch the wall. The back of the hand together with your elbow, forearm and fingers should touch the wall. The wrists should be at the same height as your shoulders.

Slowly move your hands above the head and back down about 10 times. You can do this three to five times a day.

Doing daily exercises and stretches on your neck helps prevent any injuries and pain. These stretches can also be used to reduce pain in your neck.

STRETCHES FOR NECK AND SHOULDERS

1. Flexion stretch

Push your shoulders to your back, then bring your chin down toward your chest. Bend your head forward to make it easy to stretch the neck. When done correctly, you will feel a slight stretch at the back of your neck. Hold this position for about 15 to 30 seconds.

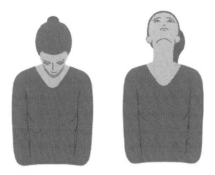

2. Lateral flexion stretch

To do this type of stretch, you need to be in your upright standing position and keep your shoulders even. Then bend your head to one side until your ear is toward the shoulder. You will feel a stretch on the side of your neck. Hold this position for 15 to 30 seconds and repeat the same process to the other side.

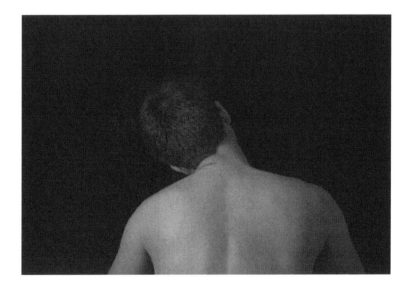

3. Corner stretch

Stand about two feet away from any corner in your house or doorway. Stand facing the corner with your feet together. Place your forearm on each of the wall or door jamb. Your elbows should be slightly below the height of your shoulders.

Lean forward until you feel a stretch on your chest and shoulders. If the stretch becomes uncomfortable, you can stop or reduce the stretch. Hold this position for about 30 to 60 seconds and repeat the same process three to five times.

4. Levator scapula stretch

You need to stand straight in this type of stretch, lift your right hand and elbow and place them on the wall or a door jamb. Remain still, and move your head to an angle of 45° toward the left. This should rotate your head halfway toward the shoulder. Hold this position for about 30 to 60 seconds or as long as you can endure, then repeat the same stretch on the other side.

CHAPTER SUMMARY

Neck and shoulder exercises are great for building and strengthening your neck muscles. The above exercises can help you in
releasing the tension and stiffness. Shoulder and neck bodyweight workouts can also help you reduce pains and loosen
muscle tightness, increasing your flexibility.

When starting the exercises, move at a slow pace and increase
the intensity of the exercises and duration as you progress. Make
your neck-stretching exercises part of your daily routine for
better results.

Avoid overworking your neck and shoulder muscles, as this can
result in injuries and pain. Do not stress or strain the muscles. If
a particular exercise doesn't feel right for you, don't do it.

In the next chapter, you will learn bodyweight exercises for
working out your chest muscles.

6

BODYWEIGHT EXERCISES FOR WORKING OUT CHEST AND BICEP MUSCLES

WORKING OUT YOUR CHEST (PECS) WILL HELP YOU IMPROVE your physique and stabilize your shoulder joints. Your chest muscles support all your daily body functions and act as a foundation for doing a variety of bodyweight workouts.

The pecs consist of the pectoralis major and pectoralis minor.

Pectoralis major is the large muscle that forms most of the chest muscles. This muscle type consists of the clavicular head on the upper portion and a sternal head on the lower part.

Your chest muscles control the movement of your arms up, down and across. The muscles allow you to carry out your daily activities. Some exercises, such as push-ups, require the use of chest muscles. They also allow you to burn more calories since the muscles can handle more weight.

Chest muscles act as a warm-up on working out the smaller muscles. Different types of exercises strengthen your chest muscles and work on your arms and shoulder muscles. Chest muscles help improve your posture, lengthen your chest and support deep breathing.

In addition to working on your back and shoulder muscles, chest muscles help improve your breathing.

EXERCISES TO BUILD CHEST MUSCLES

1. Traditional push-up

Push-ups are great for working on your chest and arms. You can do the push-up from anywhere and at any time. It needs only a firm surface and your body weight.

Push-ups work on several small muscle groups and requires you to engage your core and hip flexor muscles.

Place your hands on the floor and ensure they're shoulder-width apart. Brace your abs and keep your body in a straight line. Lower yourself down until you're a few inches off the floor and squeeze the shoulder blades together.

You can perform a wide push-up where your hands are placed wider apart than the standard shoulder-width for more variation. A wide push-up puts more pressure on your chest because more weight is transferred to your pectoral muscles. It will also help you strengthen your upper body.

2. Decline push-ups

This is a variation of the traditional push-up. In this, you put your feet on a higher ground than your hands. For example, you can place your feet on a bench, a box, or a chair. The higher the level, the more intense the exercise gets. You may find it challenging to do initially, but once you master the movement, you'll be able to easily do them, and this will get you better results.

3. Diamond push-ups

Diamond push-ups are another variation for doing more intense exercises. Put your hands close together so that your thumb and index finger touch each other to form a diamond shape. Once your hands are in position, do the push-ups.

This movement will work on your triceps and the inner chest muscles. You can do seven to 10 reps to get better results.

4. Push-up hold

A push-up hold is an isometric form of exercise strengthening your core, shoulder and arm muscles. It makes you strong—not only physically but also mentally.

In this type of workout, you hold your body up in the basic push-up position for as long as you can. Holding in the lowered position can be difficult for those who find it challenging to do the basic push-up position.

The push-up hold enables you to push your limits. The key to your success depends on your belief.

5. Dive-bomber push-up

Start by getting into a push-up position. Put your hands on the floor and raise your hips into the air. Keep your back straight and your head behind your hands.

Lower your body to be in arcing motion and your chest a few inches off the floor. Push your body forward until your torso is vertical, while your legs are straight on the floor.

6. Star plank

Star plank movement works on your chest and arm muscles. Start by getting into a push-up position. Move your hands and feet to be wide apart such that your body makes a star shape.

Hold that position for as long as you can. Keep your torso straight and brace your abs.

7. Plank reach under

Get into a plank position with your arms placed within shoulder-width (beneath your shoulders). While still in the plank position, lift your left arm and touch your right knee. Then get back to the plank position and repeat the same using the right arm.

Alternate your arms to do eight to 10 reps without any rest.

8. Side plank

In a side plank, you engage your shoulder and bicep muscles.

Start this movement with your right side. Place your right hand on the floor and extend your arm so that it forms a straight line from your ankles up to the shoulders.

Lift the left leg to ensure only the sides of your right foot and the palm of your right hand touch the floor. Hold that position for as long as you can.

Repeat the same step on your left side.

You can modify this movement by placing your forearm on the floor instead of the palms of your hand.

9. Chaturanga

Chaturanga is a classic yoga move, and you can use it to work on your biceps and core muscles.

Start by getting into a standard plank position with your hands on the floor and elbows beneath your shoulders at an angle of 90°. Lower yourself down to be a few inches off the floor. Push your elbows to be at the same height as your sides.

The move also helps work on your toe muscles. For better results, align your chest, elbows, upper arms and shoulders. Then push yourself back to the plank position and repeat the movement.

10. Resistance band biceps curl

Pick your resistance band or a towel and sit on the floor. Tuck your knees under you and straighten your spine.

Take your resistance band and slide it under your right knee. Grab it using your hand and pull it toward your right shoulder. Ensure your right arm stays in place.

Release the hold and repeat the same steps on your left knee.

CHAPTER SUMMARY

Building your chest muscles doesn't require you to use equipment or go to the gym. You can do the exercises at home and build a bigger chest. Your bodyweight will act as your equipment. You don't need complicated exercises to build your chest muscles.

Some of the above exercises not only work on your pectoralis major and minor, but they also target your abs, deltoids, triceps and other types of muscles. They help you get the best muscles you would want to show off at the beach.

In the next chapter, you will learn exercises you can use to build your core and back.

7

BODYWEIGHT EXERCISES TO WORK ON YOUR CORE AND BACK MUSCLES

EXERCISING YOUR CORE AND BACK MUSCLES HELPS YOU strengthen the key muscles that cause hunched shoulders and reduce back pain. Doing the right type of exercises increase your blood flow on your lower back and reduce stiffness.

Bodyweight exercises require high levels of core stability. To have a stable core, you need to work both abs and back muscles together. Otherwise, you will not get strong by merely focusing on a single muscle.

Your body weight is enough to work out your back and core muscles. Although some movements require you to pull up bars and straps but the only resistance you need to work against comes from your body weight.

You should also come up with a perfect workout plan for your back and core. And do a warm-up before you begin any exercise to activate your deep core muscles. A warm-up helps you get the best out of the exercises and also prevent injuries.

SIMPLE EXERCISES FOR YOUR BACK AND CORE MUSCLES

1. Low plank

Lie on your stomach with your hands extended forward, then bend your elbows to be at 90° and place your forearms on the floor. Your elbows should be directly beneath your shoulders.

Extend your legs, ensure your toes touch the floor, and slowly lift your body off the floor. Your hips and thighs should be parallel to the floor. This movement allows you to engage your core muscles and ensures that the body maintains a straight line from head to feet.

You can tuck your pelvis under to have a flat back. Ensure your lower back doesn't sag or lift.

To increase the movement's intensity, you can pull the shoulder blades in and down and hold them in that position as long as you can. Get back to the plank position and repeat the movement.

2. High plank

Get into a standard plank position with your hands placed shoulder-width apart on the floor and slightly bend your elbows.

Extend your legs and rest your toes on the floor.

Lift your hips and thighs to be diagonal to the floor. Engage the core muscles so that your body is straight from head to feet.

Tuck in your pelvis to form a flat back. Do not sag or lift your lower back or the lumbar region. Then pull your shoulder blades in and down and hold for as long as you can.

3. Bridge

You have to lie on your back with your face up and your head on the floor for this bridge exercise. Bend your knees so that your heels are directly beneath your knees. Keep your hands on your sides near your hips with your palms facing down to add balance.

Tuck your pelvis region to have a flat lower back, and then pull the shoulder blades in and down and hold them in that position. Lift your hips high until fully extended, then hold that position for about 10 seconds. Your knees, hips, and shoulders should be in a straight line. While on it, squeeze your glutes, then lower your hips back to a few inches off the floor.

Repeat the movement.

4. Superman

Superman is another bodyweight exercise that works on your upper and lower back, abs, core muscles, glutes and shoulders. Start by lying flat on your stomach with your hands stretched forward, palms placed on the floor.

Raise your legs and upper body off the floor to form an arch-like shape. Your knees and chest shouldn't touch the floor. Raise your head and tuck in your chin, and don't overextend your neck.

Extend your hands forward. You can also slightly bend the elbows as you extend them. You can increase the core tension by slightly raising the upper body and legs higher at the same time.

When doing the superman move, don't look up, as this can make you stretch your neck, making you feel uncomfortable. Make sure you lie on a yoga mat or carpet to ensure you're comfortable doing this exercise.

You can also do a variation of the W superman and T superman exercises. In the W-shape variation, squeeze the upper back and bend your arms to form a W-like shape when lifted.

While in the W superman, extend your arms out on either side of your chest to form the T shape.

5. Pull-up superman/prone pull

In a pull-up superman movement, you lie on your chest with your palms on the sides of your chest and in line with your head.

Squeeze your glutes and lower back to enable you to raise your arms and top of the chest a few inches off the floor, and your arms forming the 'W' like shape.

Extend your hands straight out and squeeze your back to pull the arms back to your chest. This movement mimics a pull-up motion. Then extend your arms out again to lower your body and complete one rep.

Get back to the starting position and do more reps before you drop your arms and legs. You can start with a few reps and increase your intensity until you can do three sets of 10 reps.

6. Cobra pose

A cobra pose helps you strengthen your ab, back and leg muscles. Start by lying face down with your hands spread on the floor. You can keep your elbows tightly tucked next to your body.

Firmly press your hips and legs on the floor. Straighten your hands while lifting your torso. Hold that position for about 15 to 30 seconds, then go back to the starting position.

Do not strain your elbows or lift higher than you can. Go slowly until you can do three sets of three to five reps simultaneously.

7. Pull-up

In this, grab your pull-up bar with a firm grip with your palms facing forward. Ensure your arms are straight, then pull yourself up the bar until the chest is directly at the bar.

This will help you strengthen your arms then slowly lower yourself down to the starting position. When you lower yourself down, your elbows should be straight, then repeat the same movement for several reps.

8. T-push-up

In this, you can start either by getting into a push-up or plank position. Place your hands a few inches outside your chest.

Squeeze your core and glutes to ensure your spine is in a straight line. Slightly bend the elbow to push your chest down. At the same time, squeeze your back at the bottom of that movement.

As you push back up to T-shape, squeeze your chest and rotate your body up on one side while raising your other arm straight up at the same time. Hold yourself up at that position, then lower yourself back to the starting position. Repeat the movement on the other side of your body.

9. Quadruple limb raise

Start by getting into a plank position (on all fours). Ensure your hands are placed shoulder-width apart on the floor. Bend your knee to be directly beneath your hips, and the body parallels to the floor.

Extend your right hand forward and the left leg backward while raised off the floor. Ensure your back is in a straight line from the head to your buttocks. Hold that position for about five to 10 seconds and then lower yourself back to the starting position. Repeat the movement on the other side.

10. Knee-to-chest stretches

Knee-to-chest exercises help to relieve any pain and tension in your lower back. To do this exercise, lie on your back with your head touching the floor.

Keep one foot flat on the floor while bending the knee of the other leg. Use both hands to pull the knee toward your chest. Hold it against the chest for about five seconds. Ensure your abdomen is kept tight and your spine is pressed on the floor.

Lower your leg back to the starting position and do the same with the other leg. You can repeat the movement in each leg two to three times.

11. Lower back rotational stretch

This is another excellent bodyweight workout that relieves tension on your lower back and works on your core muscles, as well as increases your stability.

Lie back on your yoga mat and bent your knees with your feet placed flat. Keep your shoulders on the floor with your hands spread on your sides to form a T-shape.

Roll your bent knees to one side and hold that position for five to 10 seconds.

Get back to the starting position, roll the bent knees on the opposite side and hold onto that position again. Repeat the movement to work on your lower back and core muscles.

This type of exercise uses a suspension cable. You can do it without the suspension cable and spread your hands on your sides to form the T-shape.

12. Pelvic tilts

Pelvic tilt exercises work on your tight back muscles and make them more flexible. Start by lying on your back on the mat with your knees bent and flat on the surface. Keep the arms to your side and arch your lower back gently. Push out your stomach and hold that position for five seconds.

Flatten your back, then pull your belly button toward the floor and hold that position for five seconds. As you master the move, increase the number of reps you do at a time.

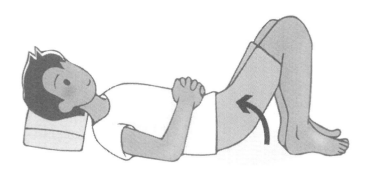

13. Reverse crunch

The reverse crunch is another bodyweight exercise you can use to work on your core muscles. It is excellent for working on your abdomen muscles.

To do this type of exercise, lie down on your back with your face up. Bent your knees at 90° with your feet placed flat on the floor. Keep your arms on your sides with the palms down.

Lift your feet off the floor, raise your thighs until they're vertical, and ensure your knees are still bent at 90°.

Push your knees toward your face, tuck them as far as you can go. Do not lift your mid-back off the floor. Only your lower back and hips should be lifted off the floor.

Hold that position for a few seconds, then lower your feet back until they touch the floor. Repeat the movement until you're able to do 10 to 12 reps. You can start with a single set and increase the sets and reps you do as you get stronger.

CHAPTER SUMMARY

Working on your core and back muscles makes you more flexible, prevents injuries, and improves your stability. If you experience back pain often, these types of exercises can help you relieve your condition.

The above exercises are easy to do and are used by both beginners and advanced fitness fanatics. You can begin with a few reps, and as you get stronger, you can increase the number of reps and sets done.

Always make sure you do the exercises correctly. Otherwise, you will be doing more harm than obtaining the desired benefits. If you experience some pain when doing the exercise, you can stop and try it another day. Do not strain your muscles.

Although the exercises can solve various health issues, if you're experiencing severe pain that can't be solved with exercise, please see a doctor.

In the next chapter, you will learn bodyweight exercises to work on your thighs and the large leg muscles.

8

BODYWEIGHT EXERCISES FOR WORKING THIGH MUSCLES

THIGHS AND LEGS HAVE THE LARGEST MUSCLE GROUPS compared to other parts of your body. You can do various bodyweight exercises to target the calves, glutes, hamstrings and quads.

If you're consistent with the workouts, you can notice the changes within a week or two.

Your thigh has three fascial compartments that house about 18 muscles. These muscles are responsible for your knee's rotation, flexion, extension and abduction of your hips.

Since your thighs have more muscle mass, engaging in various workouts that target thigh muscles will help burn more calories even when sitting down.

Strengthening your thigh muscles makes it easy for you to walk, ride bicycles and even climb stairs. They also help you improve your resting metabolic rate.

The muscles found on your thighs and hips helps you maintain an erect posture and enable rotation of your thighs outward.

THIGH AND LEGS EXERCISES

1. Squats

Squats are one of the best workouts that engage your core, glutes and quads. Squats ensure you have healthy and firm thighs and legs.

Stand with your feet shoulder-width apart and lower your hips down as if you want to sit down. As you lower your hips, bend your knees to 45° and your thighs parallel to the floor.

The depth you can bend your knees varies from one person to the other. This is because the depth depends on one's lower body strength, anatomy and mobility.

Lift yourself and repeat this movement for eight to 10 reps.

2. Jump squat

Jump squat is a modified squat that increases the intensity of your workout. It works on your fast-twitch muscle fibers found in your legs and increases your heart rate. As a result, you're able to burn more calories.

Just like in a regular squat move, instead of raising to start position slowly, you add an explosive jump to get back straight up, then land softly and quietly to your starting position.

Once you get into a squat position so that your thighs are parallel to the floor, you can then have an explosive jump as high as you can. When landing, you can bend your knees to be at 45°. Get into another squat position and hold there for a second before you jump again.

3. Sumo squat

Sumo squat is another variation of squat that engages your hip muscles and works on your quads and glutes. Stand with your feet placed wider apart than shoulder-width. Turn your toes slightly out like a sumo wrestler.

Maintain an upright posture and lower your hips down toward your heels while driving your knees out. When squatting down, make sure your knees are kept behind your toes while the shin is maintained vertically at the bottom of the squat.

Slowly stand up by pushing your heels down and out, then push your hips forward to an extended position.

4. Side lunge

Put your feet wide apart (twice shoulder-width apart). Push your hips to the back and the left side. Keep your right leg straight when moving the hips. Bend the left knee, lower your body so that your left thigh is in a parallel position with the floor.

Ensure your feet are flat on the floor when doing the movements. Hold that position for at least two seconds before getting back. Complete reps and switch to the other side.

5. Jump lunge

Just like in a jump squat, you can do a jump to a lunge workout. This is an advanced form of lunge exercise, so master the lunge exercise before doing the jump lunge.

Jump lunge works on your fast-twitch muscle fibers that burn fat in your body and increase your heart rate.

To do this exercise, get into a standard lunge position. Once you lower yourself down into lunge position, jump up, then switch your legs so that the opposite leg is at the front when you land. You should land softly and quietly.

LUNGE JUMP

6. Glute bridge

If you have an injury and find it difficult to squat or do a lunge, you can do a glute bridge exercise. This type of bodyweight exercise activates your glutes, hamstrings and lower back muscles.

Lie down on your back with your head touching the floor. Bend your knees and place your feet flat on the floor to about shoulder-width apart. Then raise your hips off the floor while pushing your heels down onto the floor.

Once your hips are higher up, squeeze your glute, and tighten your abdominal muscle. This prevents you from arching your lower back. Keep the shins vertical and hold that position for two seconds, then lower yourself back to the starting position.

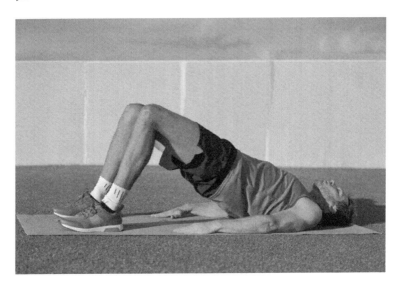

7. Single-leg glute bridge

Lie down face up with your arms out on your sides. Bend your right foot and firmly place the heel of your foot on the ground and extend your left leg to be straight.

Activate your abs and contract your glute muscles to enable you to push your hips up into the bridge position and then lift your left leg off the floor and in line with your right thigh.

While at the top, squeeze glute muscles and then lower yourself back down. Your left leg should be off the floor when doing all reps. Switch legs and repeat the same steps.

You can also use a suspension trainer to increase the intensity of this type of workout.

8. Supine leg curl

Lie with your back on the floor, and place your feet on a slippery object like a towel or some socks. Lift your hips off the floor, extend your legs straight forward, and slightly pull your heels back under your body.

This type of exercise puts more pressure on your hamstrings muscles and adds more flexion and extension to your knee. It also works on your glutes and lower back muscles.

CHAPTER SUMMARY

Exercising your thigh and leg muscles helps you in correcting any muscle imbalance and injuries. The exercise can also tighten your lower back and strengthen your core.

Including several exercises in your workout routine allow you to focus on a particular group of muscles and improve your overall well-being. Most people tend to neglect their leg muscles and only work out the upper body muscles. But, to have a healthy, balanced, and stable body, you need to include your leg and thigh muscles in your fitness plan.

Be consistent with the exercises because the large leg muscles form an integral part of your fitness goals. Working on this group of muscles keeps your body balanced and makes it easy to work on your upper body muscles. They also help you boost your athletic performance.

Do not overtrain your muscles and balance your exercise routine to focus on both glutes and hamstrings.

FINAL WORDS

Bodyweight exercises are essential to build your muscle mass and strengthen your cardiovascular system and nervous system. You don't need any equipment or subscribe to a gym to maintain your fitness goals.

You can do the exercises from anywhere and at any time. You can easily do the exercises in the comfort of your home or even in your office. There are so many reasons why you should include bodyweight exercises in your fitness journey.

These exercises are cost-effective, time-efficient, highly scalable, safe, flexible, and can easily combine cardio and strength training. Strength-training exercises help you increase your body image, improve your body mechanism, boost your energy levels, manage chronic health diseases, burn fat and build lean muscles.

A whole-body workout helps you to be more flexible, effectively lose weight, increase your endurance level, improve your balance, and reduce the risk of injuries and pains.

The exercises rely on your bodyweight to provide you with the resistance needed for the movements. To achieve the desired results, you need to be consistent with the workouts.

If you're looking forward to increasing muscle mass, you have to do the exercises quickly and make the muscles more explosive.

Also, it helps to focus on the strength-training principles to achieve the desired results: Simplicity, individualism, progression and overload. Always focus on a specific type of exercise to work on certain kinds of muscles, especially if you have limited time.

Stick to what works for you. Our bodies are different, so if specific exercises work for your friend, it doesn't mean it will work for you. Start with simple steps. Once your body gets used to the exercises, you can increase your workload, time and resistance. Increasing your workload with the right rest time will result in an overload.

Before starting any exercise, you need to have a warm-up session of at least five to 10 minutes. If you're targeting a specific muscle, do a warm-up to activate those muscles before beginning the actual workout. You should also avoid overtraining to avoid any injuries and exhaustion.

When planning to start your workout routine, you need to check your health and then develop your workout plan. The workout plan helps you determine your fitness level that works as your benchmark to compare your progress.

After knowing your body composition, muscle density and flexibility, you can develop your fitness program. You need to decide your fitness goals, type of exercises to do, and what muscle groups on which to work.

Create a balanced routine to help you achieve your goals. Incorporate the exercises into your daily routine. Include different types of activities, as well as incorporate high-intensity exercises and recovery time. Avoid doing the exercises continuously without any rest. This can result in injuries or joint pains.

Assemble all the tools you need for your exercise. For example, have a yoga mat, a tracking device, sports shoes and others.

Start slow with simple steps and proceed gradually. If you have a busy schedule, you can break down the exercises to have several sessions of exercises per day. You can incorporate several numbers of exercises to do per week. You don't have to limit yourself to a few of them.

Pay more attention to your body. How do you feel after every exercise? If you have been pushing yourself too much, then it's time to slow down and take a break.

Monitor your progress every month to know whether you're on the right track. Can you achieve your fitness goals with the current phase? If not, you should increase your exercise time or intensity of the workout to obtain measurable benefits.

If you didn't achieve your fitness goals, don't give up. Just set up new goals and new exercise activities to do. You can also include your family and friends in the exercises to have more fun.

You should also determine workout days and rest days. You should be consistent to achieve the desired results. Your workout plan should have high-intensity workouts followed by recovery days with light exercises and rest days.

Based on your fitness goals, you can choose the number of sets and reps you're supposed to do on each type of exercise.

After deciding on your workout plan, it is time to start your exercises that target different muscle types. For example, body-weight exercises that target upper body muscles like your arms muscles.

Exercises that strengthen your arms target your shoulders, biceps and triceps. These exercises engage your core and allow you to work on different muscles simultaneously. You don't need any equipment to do the exercises.

All you need is a proper workout plan and flexing the muscles of your forearms and triceps. Some of the typical bodyweight workouts for arms include dips, tricep dips with lifted legs, pull-ups, chin-ups, plank, up-and-down plank, push-ups, and inch-worm with shoulder taps, among others. These exercises not only build muscles but also help you in burning calories.

You also need to work on your neck and shoulder muscles. Neck and shoulders are incredibly mobile, and some motions may leave you with some pain or injuries. Thus, the need to strengthen your neck and shoulder muscles.

Working out your neck and shoulder muscles makes you more flexible and improves your overall body structure. The exercises also help prevent injuries on your delicate areas, such as the shoulder joints.

Shoulder and neck exercises work on your rotator cuff and deltoid muscles. Some of the best exercises you can include in your plan include incline push-up, push-back push-up, plank to down dog, elevated pike push-up, plank up, wall walk, crab walk, reverse burpees, etc.

You can also incorporate neck-stretching exercises to relieve any neck pain and strengthen the neck muscles. Stretching and exercising the neck muscles will improve your posture and leave your head in a neutral position.

Different types of exercises target different neck muscles, including a variety of exercises in your neck workout. This includes exercise, such as chin tuck, prone cobra, and back burn.

Another set of muscles you need to work out is your chest and biceps. These muscles help you improve your physique and stabilize your shoulder joints.

Chest muscles are critical as they support all your daily body functions, acting as the foundation for almost all types of workouts. These muscles control the movement of your arms up, down and across.

Some of the chest workouts you can include in your workout plan include push-up, decline push-up, push-up hold, star plank, chaturanga, dive-bomber push-up, etc.

Some of these chest muscle workouts target your abs, deltoids and triceps. They enable you to get the perfect muscles you need to show off on a beach.

We also discussed various exercises you can use to work out your core and lower back muscles. These exercises help you prevent hunched shoulders and reduce back pains. Choosing the right type of exercise and the number of reps will increase your blood flow and reduce the lower back's stiffness. For better results, you need to engage your abs and back muscles together.

Exercises include the low plank, high-plank, bridge, superman, pull-up, pull-up superman, t-pushup, cobra pose, reverse crunch and pelvic tilt. You can do any of these exercises to reduce any pain and solve various health issues.

To complete your whole-body exercises, you need to work on your thigh and leg muscles. Our legs consist of the largest number of muscles and have more muscle mass.

Most of the leg workouts target your calves, glutes, hamstrings and quads. Exercises that target these different muscles help you burn more calories and improve your metabolic rate.

Exercising your thigh and leg muscles regularly enables you to tone your muscles and ensure you have strong thighs and legs. The best workouts for your legs muscles include squats, jump squats, sumo squats, side lunge, jump lunge, glute-bridge and supine leg curl.

For effective results, you have to include both simple and high intensive exercises. You can also increase the number of reps you do in each workout once you master the move. Adding some variations to the exercises enables you to increase your heart rate.

Remember to do a warm-up before beginning the exercises and some stretches after the exercises to increase your body's blood flow. Choosing the right type of activity and a proper diet will help you achieve your fitness goals.

Image Credit: Shutterstock.com

AUTHOR'S NOTE

I hope you enjoy this book as much as I loved writing it. If you do, it would be wonderful if you could take a short minute and leave a review on Amazon as soon as you can, as your kind feedback is much appreciated and so very important.

Thank you!

SPECIAL BONUS!

Get this additional Free 30 Days to Fitness Challenge Book 100% FREE!

Hundreds of others are already enjoying insider access to all of my current and future full-length books, 100% free!

If you want insider access plus this Free 30 Days to Fitness Challenge Book, all you have to do is **click the link below** to claim your offer!

https://mailchi.mp/1085fc44d91b/bodyweight-workout-for-men

REFERENCES

https://en.wikipedia.org/wiki/Calisthenics

https://www.mensjournal.com/health-fitness/how-to-build-muscle-without-lifting-weights/

https://www.ownyoureating.com/blog/10-reasons-why-bodyweight-training-is-the-best-form-of-exercise/

https://www.realbuzz.com/articles-interests/fitness/article/the-four-principles-of-training/

https://www.womenshealthmag.com/fitness/a30522035/what-is-strength-training/

https://www.healthline.com/health/fitness-nutrition/no-weight-workout

https://www.verywellfit.com/complete-beginners-guide-to-strength-training-1229585

https://www.healthline.com/nutrition/how-to-start-exercising#TOC_TITLE_HDR_5

https://www.mayoclinic.org/healthy-lifestyle/fitness/in-depth/fitness/art-20048269

https://www.nerdfitness.com/blog/how-to-build-your-own-workout-routine/

https://www.nerdfitness.com/blog/beginner-body-weight-workout-burn-fat-build-muscle/

https://www.mensjournal.com/health-fitness/9-best-bodyweight-moves-develop-colossal-arms/3-suspension-trainer-biceps-curls/

https://greatist.com/fitness/bodyweight-workout-for-biceps#beginner

https://www.menshealth.com/fitness/a25620352/best-bodyweight-back-exercises/

https://www.mensjournal.com/health-fitness/best-bodyweight-exercises-legs/15-swiss-ball-wall-squat/

Printed in Great Britain
by Amazon